JUMP THE WORLD

Stories, Poems, and Things to Make and Do from Around the World

by Sarah Pooley

DUTTON CHILDREN'S BOOKS

NEW YORK

⭐ Acknowledgments ⭐

Thanks are due to the following for permission to reprint the material listed below:

"The Two Parrots," "The Wedding Gift," "The Captain's Goose," "Peter and the Wolf," "The Story of the Willow Pattern Plate," and "The Monkey and the Crocodile," retold by Alison Green, copyright © 1997 by Macmillan Children's Books. Reprinted by permission of Macmillan Children's Books.
"Banana Man," from *Come On into my Tropical Garden* by Grace Nichols. Reprinted by permission of Curtis Brown Group Ltd, London, on behalf of Grace Nichols. Copyright © 1988 by Grace Nichols.
"The Fabulous Spotted Egg," from *Myths and Legends*, retold by Anthony Horowitz. Copyright © 1985 by Anthony Horowitz. Reprinted by permission of Kingfisher Books.
"I want my breakfast," from *Blackberry Ink* by Eve Merriam. Copyright © 1985 by Eve Merriam. Reprinted by permission of Marian Reiner. Published by Morrow Junior Books and available in paperback.
"An African ABC" (original title: "An Azanian Abecedarius") by Tessa Welch. Reprinted by permission of Abecedarius Books/Hippogriff Press.
"The Pelican" (original title: "Le Pélican") by Robert Desnos, from *Chantefables et Chantefleurs*, copyright © by Librairie Gründ. English translation by Alison Green, copyright © 1997 by Macmillan Children's Books.
"Shrewd Todie and Lyzer the Miser," from *Stories for Children* by Isaac Bashevis Singer. Copyright © 1984 by Isaac Bashevis Singer. Translated by the author and Elizabeth Shub. Reprinted by permission of Farrar, Straus & Giroux, Inc. Abridged by Alison Green.
Haiku from *The Penguin Book of Zen Poetry*, translated by Lucien Stryk. Reprinted by permission of the translator.
"Waltzing Matilda" by A. B. "Banjo" Patterson. Copyright © 1936, 1941 by Carl Fischer, Inc. Copyrights renewed. All rights reserved. Reprinted by permission.

All text for activities and recipes copyright © 1997 by Sarah Pooley. Reprinted by permission of Macmillan Children's Books.

Every effort has been made to trace the copyright holders of the material in this book, and the publisher apologizes for any inadvertent omissions.

Compilation and illustrations copyright © Sarah Pooley, 1997
All rights reserved.

CIP Data is available.

Published in the United States 1997 by Dutton Children's Books,
a division of Penguin Books USA Inc.
375 Hudson Street, New York, New York 10014

Originally published in Great Britain 1997 by Macmillan Children's Books, London

Typography by Semadar Megged and Richard Amari
Printed in Hong Kong   First American Edition
ISBN 0-525-45798-4

CONTENTS

Don't forget . . .

When you are doing any of the activities or recipes from this book:

- Make sure you have everything you will need before you start.
- If you are cooking, wash your hands first.
- Put an apron on before starting any cooking, painting, or gluing.
- If you are using paint or glue, cover your entire work surface with old newspapers first.
- Spray sealant outside the house or in a well-ventilated room.
- Always ask an adult to help you if you are using sharp knives or scissors, or if you need to use the stove.
- Always put everything away when you have finished—and wash the dishes, too!

The Two Parrots

The Sun was out hunting one day when he found two parrots. Thinking that they would make fine pets, he took them home. He kept the one with the brightest feathers for himself and gave the other to his brother, the Moon, who was also in the form of a young man.

Sun and Moon took great care of the parrots and would spend hours stroking their plumage and teaching them to talk. In return, the parrots grew very fond of their masters.

One day, when Sun and Moon were out hunting, one of the parrots said to the other, "It makes me sad to see our masters work so hard all day with their hunting, and then come home tired and have to prepare their food before they can rest. They will wear themselves out."

The second parrot agreed, and the two birds decided to see what they could do to help.

The next day, the birds waited until their masters had left the hut and were out of sight. Then, in an instant, the birds turned into young girls. They set to work immediately, preparing an evening meal for Sun and Moon. The girls took turns working, one of them always keeping watch by the door so that if the men should return early they would have time to turn back into parrots.

At dusk, Sun and Moon returned home, weary from their day's hunting. They were still some distance away when they heard a strange noise coming from their hut—a heavy pounding noise, as if a huge animal were moving around. They approached stealthily, puzzled as to what it might be. When they were quite near, Sun exclaimed, "That is no animal—it sounds like a huge pestle crushing corn! Who could be pounding corn inside our hut?"

They ran toward the hut, hoping to catch the intruder. But as they reached the door, the noise stopped. Moon flung the door open, and the brothers searched the hut. There was no one to be seen except the parrots, sleeping on their perch, but on the table were two freshly made bowls of cornmeal.

Sun and Moon were amazed. They searched high and low but found no one in the hut. "Maybe the parrots cooked our supper!" said Sun, laughing, and the parrots cawed loudly, as if enjoying the joke.

Then Moon spotted some footprints on the hut's mud floor—small, delicate footprints that crisscrossed the ground in front of the fire. The brothers followed the tracks to see where the intruders had entered, but to their great puzzlement the prints never once crossed the threshold of the hut. "Who has been here?" Moon asked the parrots. But the birds looked innocently at him and said nothing.

The cornmeal was good, and the brothers thought it was a fine thing to have their supper already prepared for them, so that night they thought no more about it. They slept well and set off to hunt the next day, much refreshed.

Every day after that the same thing happened, and the

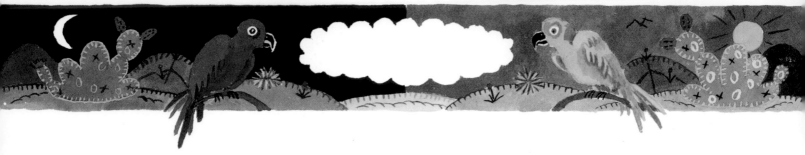

brothers grew used to finding their hut tidied and their supper waiting for them in the evening.

But Sun still wanted to find out the answer to the mystery, so one day he said to Moon, "Let us pretend today that we are going out hunting as usual. But instead of going into the forest, we will hide nearby. As soon as we hear the pounding of the pestle on the corn, we'll burst into the hut and catch the intruder red-handed."

"Good idea," said Moon.

The brothers acted as if that day were like any other, preparing their hunting gear with care and stroking the parrots' heads before they strode off toward the forest. But before they reached the forest they turned, crept back by a different route, and hid behind some trees near the hut.

At first, all they could hear was the noise of the parrots chattering to each other. Then the chattering was replaced by the sound of girls' voices, laughing and talking, and a few minutes later they heard the familiar pounding of the pestle.

In an instant, the brothers raced back to the hut and flung open the door. The two girls had no time to turn back into parrots. They simply put down the pestle and looked calmly at the astonished young men.

Sun and Moon were dumbstruck by the girls beauty. Never had they seen such lovely creatures: one with hair as golden as the day, the other with hair as dark as the night sky.

As the young men seemed unable to speak, the fair-haired girl smiled and said, "Do you not know us? We are the parrots you cared for so well. We felt sorry for you, working so hard, and decided to help you. We transformed ourselves into humans so that we could cook your food."

"We can turn back into parrots if you would prefer," said the dark-haired girl.

"No!" cried Sun and Moon in unison. "Stay as you are."

"Very well," replied the girls. "Then you must decide which of us each of you wants to marry."

Without a moment's hesitation, Sun stepped forward and took the hand of the golden-haired girl. "I choose you!" he cried. "For you are more lovely than the day."

"And I will marry you!" cried Moon to the dark-haired girl. "For you are more beautiful than a night sky full of stars."

So the brothers were married, and, for a time, all four lived happily together. However, the hut was small for four people, and they soon decided to take turns staying there. Sun and his wife slept there at night, and Moon and his wife slept there by day.

And that is why the Sun always hunts by day, when his light brightens the world, while his brother, the Moon, hunts by night, carrying his bows and arrows through the stars.

Papier-Mâché Parrot Bowls

Make bowls for the Sun and the Moon. Decorate them with poster paints or with cut-up pieces of paper. Don't forget, these bowls are for decoration only—don't put anything wet in them or they will fall apart!

Recipe
1 cup of flour
2 cups of water
mix and
cook until
custard-like.
Cool

You will need:
1 or more bowls (glass, china, or plastic)
lots of torn-up strips of newspaper
wallpaper paste or flour-and-water paste
vegetable oil or Vaseline
poster paints, colored paper
water-based sealant or clear nail polish

Flourpride

Sunshine Wall paste

White Petroleum Jelly

scissors

round-ended knife

paint brushes

VARNO for varnishing

1. Rub vegetable oil or Vaseline all over the inside and rim of the bowl.
2. Cover both sides of a strip of newspaper with paste and stick it on the inside of the bowl.

3. Repeat with other strips of newspaper until the inside of the bowl is covered with one layer of paper. Allow to dry.

4. Paste a second layer of newspaper strips over the first and again allow it to dry. Repeat until you have built up at least seven layers of newspaper. The more layers you have, the stronger your finished bowl will be.

5. Leave the bowl in a warm place for three days to dry completely.

6. Slide a knife between the newspaper and the bowl to loosen it, then gently ease the papier-mâché out of the bowl.

7. Trim around the rim of the papier-mâché bowl with scissors. Paste over the cut edge with two layers of small strips of newspaper and allow to dry.

8. Paint the bowl inside and out with poster paint. When it is dry, paint a design on the bowl, or glue on pieces of colored paper to decorate it.

9. When all the paint or glue has dried, brush or spray a water-based sealant all over the bowl to protect it.

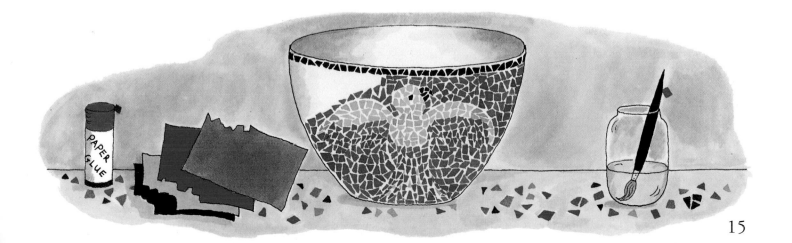

THE CARIBBEAN

Banana Man

GRACE NICHOLS

I'm a banana man
I just love shaking
those yellow hands
Yes, man
Banana in the morning
Banana in the evening
Banana before I go to bed
at night—that's right
that's how much I love
the banana bite

I'm a banana man
not a superman
or a batman
or a spiderman
No, man
Banana in the morning
Banana in the evening
Banana before I go to bed
at night—that's right
that's how much I love
the banana bite

Caribbean Baked Bananas

You will need:

6 bananas
½ teaspoon ground nutmeg
½ teaspoon ground cinnamon
2–3 tablespoons brown sugar
2 tablespoons butter or margarine
½ cup fresh orange juice

large baking dish
bowl
knife
spoon

1. Ask an adult to set the oven to 350° F.
2. Use a little butter or margarine to grease the inside of the baking dish.
3. Cut the bananas in half lengthwise and place them in the baking dish.
4. In a bowl, mix the orange juice with the nutmeg, cinnamon, and sugar. Pour this mixture over the bananas.
5. Cut up the remaining butter or margarine and dot it over the bananas.
6. Place the bananas in the oven and bake for 15–20 minutes.
7. Serve the bananas hot with cream, ice cream, or yogurt.

The Fabulous Spotted Egg

Retold by ANTHONY HOROWITZ

The Cheyenne Indians, who rode the plains of North America in the seventeenth and eighteenth centuries, had a strange custom. Whenever they came to a wide stretch of water—a lake or a river, perhaps—they would throw some food or tobacco in before they rode across. Nobody asked the Cheyennes why they did this, but there was a very good reason. It was contained in a tale told by the Cheyenne storytellers—a tale about a great river monster and two brothers who discovered a fabulous spotted egg.

The two brothers—their names aren't known, but we'll call them Elder and Younger—had managed to get themselves lost on the prairie. The horizon made a great big circle all around them and there was nothing to see except the grass, waving in the wind. The brothers had a little water, but they had no food.

They walked a few miles, getting hungrier and hungrier. Soon the rumble of their stomachs accompanied the rustle of the wind. Then all of a sudden they came upon an egg—just lying on the ground with no sign of a bird or a nest anywhere near.

"Well, that's a stroke of luck," Younger said. "Look at that egg. I bet it will last the two of us a whole week."

"I'm not so sure," Elder growled. "It doesn't look too healthy to me."

"What do you mean?" Younger cried. "It's just an egg."

But if it was just an egg, it was just a very peculiar egg. For a start it was bright green with red spots. Also it was enormous—much bigger than a chicken egg. Much bigger, in fact, than a chicken. And how had it gotten there? It was, after all, in the middle of the prairie.

"It looks magic to me," Elder said. "I say we don't touch it."

"Come on!" Younger replied. "It was probably laid by a big bird or a turtle. Okay, so it's a funny color. But I'm so hungry, I'd eat a green and red spotted horse!"

So while Elder watched, Younger lit a bonfire and roasted the egg. Then he cracked the shell and began to eat.

"You sure you don't want some?" he asked.

"No, thanks," Elder said.

"It's really good. You don't know what you're missing."

In fact, Younger was lying when he said that. The egg was hard and rubbery. The yolk was green, the same color as the shell, and the white wasn't white but a sort of pink. And it didn't taste like an egg should. It tasted like fish.

Even as Younger ate he began to feel sick, but something made him go on eating. He couldn't stop. Faster and faster he spooned the egg into his mouth until only the shell was left.

"I hope you know what you're doing," Elder muttered.

When he woke up the next morning, Younger was feeling very sick. His stomach felt like a carnival merry-go-round and his eyes were as big as Ping-Pong balls. Worst of all, he was terribly thirsty. He drank all the water in his leather pouch, but it could have been a thimbleful for all the good it did him. Elder looked at him and sighed.

"You look terrible," he said.

"I feel terrible," Younger agreed.

"You're green!"

"Green?"

"And you've got red spots."

Younger stood up. "Let's go!" he said. "The sooner we find water the better. I need a drink."

They walked until sunset, by which time Younger's skin had become greener and his spots even redder. All his hair had fallen out and he seemed to be having trouble talking.

"Sssssay," he hissed. "Do you think I made a misssssstake eating that egg?"

"I'm afraid so, kid," Elder replied, looking worried.

"I guesssss it was kind of sssssstupid. But I'll feel better when I get to the water. I really want a ssssswim."

The next morning Younger was much worse. His arms had somehow glued themselves to his sides and his nose had dropped off. He was a vivid green and red and his skin was as shiny as a snake's.

"I feel worsssssse," he moaned.

"You look worse," Elder said.

"I must have water!"

They reached a river at sunset. Younger, whose legs had almost melted into each other, decided that he would rather sleep in the river while Elder curled up on land beside a bonfire. Elder hadn't eaten for five days and he was weak and tired. It didn't take him long to fall asleep.

He was awakened by the sound of singing. When he opened his eyes, the first thing he saw was a great heap of fish lying on the bank, waiting to be cooked. Then he looked beyond, in the water, and saw his brother.

Except that it wasn't really his brother anymore. The boy had become an enormous sea-monster with huge teeth, slimy scales, and a forked tail. He was swimming back and forth, stopping now and then to fork another fish with the point of his tail and flip it up onto the bank.

"Hey, kid!" Elder called out. "How are you feeling today?"

"Fine!" Younger replied. "It'sssss not sssso bad being a sssssea-sssssserpent. And I've caught a whole lot of fisssssh!"

"Thanks!" Elder said.

"Hey—lisssssten," Younger continued. "Don't you forget about me. I found something for you to eat, sssso you get me food, too. I don't want to eat fissssh all my life."

"I won't forget," Elder promised.

"And tobacco, too. Just because I'm a monssssster, it doesn't mean I can't sssssmoke!"

And that is why the Cheyennes always stopped to throw food or tobacco into a river before they crossed it—even when they were being chased by the cavalry. It was to keep the sea-serpent singing.

Make a Fabulous Spotted Egg

You will need:

1 egg (white, if possible)
darning needle or large safety pin
bowl
newspaper

1 tablespoon turmeric
blue ink (or green Easter egg dye)
red tempera or poster paint
water-based sealant
paintbrushes

Blow an egg and make it fabulously spotted!

1. Cover your work surface with newspaper and place the bowl on it.

2. Carefully make a small hole at one end of the egg with a needle or safety pin. Move the needle around until the hole is 1/4 inch across. Do the same at the other end of the egg.

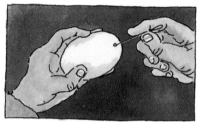

3. Break up the egg yolk with the needle.

4. Remove the needle, hold the egg over the bowl, and blow gently through one end. Keep blowing until all the egg white and yolk are in the bowl. Gently rinse out the eggshell with cold water.

5. To make a green color, mix one tablespoon of turmeric in hot water and add a few drops of blue ink, or follow the instructions on an Easter egg kit. Put the eggshell into the green dye for 30 minutes. Remove it with a spoon and allow it to dry.

6. Paint some red spots on it.

7. When the paint is dry, spray the egg all over with a clear, water-based sealant.

8. If you don't want to blow the egg out, you can hard-boil it and then dye and paint it, but it will only keep for about three days in the fridge.

UNITED STATES OF AMERICA
"I want my breakfast"
EVE MERRIAM

"I want my breakfast,"
The giant said,
"The minute that I wake up
In my giant bed.

"Tell the kitchen,"
The giant said,
"I'm giantly hungry,
And I better get fed.

"I don't want oatmeal
Or eggs with toast.
I want what I want
And I want it the most.

"One hundred pancakes
And not one less,
And enough maple syrup
To make a giant mess."

The Giant's Pancakes

To make 12 pancakes you will need:

1 ½ cups all-purpose flour
1 tablespoon sugar
½ teaspoon baking powder
2 cups milk
½ teaspoon vanilla
2 large eggs
2 tablespoons melted butter

sieve or flour sifter
mixing bowl
small pitcher or bowl
whisk or fork
small saucepan
tablespoon and teaspoon
8-inch frying pan
metal spatula
plates
dishcloth or aluminum foil

Anybody at home?!

Jack and the Beanstalk

1. Sift together the flour, sugar, and baking powder into the mixing bowl.

2. Mix the milk and vanilla together in a small pitcher or bowl.

3. Make a well in the center of the flour mixture and break the eggs into it.

4. Start whisking the eggs, adding a little of the flour from around the edges.

5. Start adding the milk mixture to the eggs a little at a time. Keep whisking and bringing the flour into the center of the bowl until all the flour has been absorbed by the liquid and you have added all of the milk.

6. Stir the mixture well so that there are no lumps. The batter should be smooth, like thin cream.

7. Melt the butter gently in a small saucepan. Add the melted butter to the pancake batter and stir well.

8. Place the frying pan on the stove and turn the heat up high. Put a teaspoon of butter into the pan and swirl it around so that the pan is greased all over.

9. When the pan is really hot, turn the heat down to medium.

10. Place two tablespoons of batter in the pan and quickly tip it so that the batter spreads evenly over the base of the pan.

11. After a minute or two, carefully lift the edge of the pancake with a metal spatula. If the pancake is a light golden color, it is cooked on that side. Use the spatula to turn it over very carefully (or toss the pancake if you know how), and cook the other side of the pancake for about a minute.

12. When it's cooked, slide the pancake onto a plate and cover with a dishcloth or foil to keep it warm while you make the rest of the pancakes.

13. Take one pancake and pour a little maple syrup or sprinkle powdered sugar on it. Roll it up and eat it. For a Giant Breakfast, eat ninety-nine more!

SOUTH AFRICA
An African ABC
TESSA WELCH

All of the words in this ABC poem are the names of South African animals.
According to the traditions of the Sotho (one of the peoples of South Africa), the return
of the Amasi bird brings peace and plenty to the fatherland.

Antbear, antelope, caracal, chat,
Bokmakierie, bulbul, mongoose, bat,
Coelacanth, cobra, porcupine, genet,
Dassie, dolphin, serval, civet,
Eland, elephant, hedgehog, whale,
Francolin, fish eagle, cheetah, snail,
Gemsbok, guinea fowl, wildebeest, mossie,
Hoopoe, hyena, ostrich, suni,
Impala, inyala, bateleur, kudu,
Jackal, giraffe, waterbuck, puku,
Korhaan, klipspringer, python, seal,
Legevaan, leopard, piet-my-vrou, eel,
Mamba, meerkat, bontebok, ibis,
Nagapie, nightjar, crocodile, mantis,

Oribi, octopus, sable, otter,
Phalarope, penguin, oriole, plover,
Quagga, quail, pangolin, shark,
Rhinoceros, reedbuck, kingfisher, lark,
Springbok, scorpion, polecat, hornbill,
Tsessebe, tigerfish, starling, petrel,
Ungulungu, duiker, weaverbird, adder,
Vervet, vleiloerie, cormorant, badger,
Warthog, wagtail, toktokkie, mole,
Xhama, chameleon, crayfish, sole,
Yellowtail, nyathi, rattlesnake, hippo,
Zebra, songololo, starfish, drongo—
Fish and insect, flock and herd,
Welcome the return of the Amasi bird.

African Tracks

Follow the tracks of these hoofed mammals and see if you can identify them. Where have they been?

Then help the springbok through the African savanna to find its mother.

 Springbok

 Klipspringer

 Zebra

 Giraffe

 Hippopotamus

 Rhinoceros

Arabic Proverbs

Arabic is spoken in many countries in North Africa and the Middle East, including Egypt, Jordan, Lebanon, Morocco, Saudi Arabia, and Syria. Like English, Arabic has many proverbs—traditional, often funny sayings that sometimes teach a moral lesson and sometimes just express an idea that many people believe to be true.

You will see that a lot of Arabic proverbs are very similar to English ones but use different words. Which ones do you like best?

Arabic

He married the monkey for its money. The money went, and the monkey stayed a monkey.

English

You made your bed; now you must lie in it.

Arabic

He ate the camel and all it carried.

English

He ate us out of house and home.

30

Arabic

Tomorrow there will be apricots.

English

Tomorrow never comes.

Arabic

We let him in and he brought his donkey, too.

English

Give him an inch and he'll take a mile.

Arabic

When the lions were absent, the hyenas played.

English

When the cat's away, the mice will play.

31

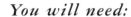 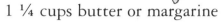

You will need:

1 cup whole wheat flour

¾ cup plain white flour

2 teaspoons baking powder

1 cup ground almonds

1 ¼ cups butter or margarine

1 ½ cups runny honey

1 teaspoon almond flavoring

4 large eggs

¾ cup milk

round 10-inch cake pan, sieve, large bowl, two smaller bowls, electric mixer or spoon, fork, knife, wire cooling rack

1. Grease the cake pan thoroughly with butter and sprinkle flour inside it.

2. Ask an adult to set the oven to 350° F.

3. Sift the flours and baking powder into a small bowl. Stir in the almonds.

4. In the large bowl, beat the butter and honey together until they are smooth and creamy. Stir in the almond flavoring.

5. In a small bowl, beat an egg and add it to the butter and honey mixture. Stir well. Add the other three eggs in the same way, one at a time.

6. Fold the flour mixture into the honey mixture. Add the milk a bit at a time, and mix well.

7. Pour the mixture into the cake pan and bake it in the lower third of the oven for 55–65 minutes. To test if it's ready, put the tip of a knife into the center of the cake. If it comes out clean, the cake is ready.

8. Let the cake cool in the pan for 10 minutes, then turn it out onto the wire rack to cool completely. Eat it as it is, or cut it in half and spread jam or honey on it.

The Story of Fidgety Philip

HEINRICH HOFFMANN

Cautionary tales like this one were very popular in the nineteenth century. The poems told children what terrible things would happen to them if they didn't behave.

"Philip, see if you are able
To sit still for once at table."
Papá thus bade Phil behave;
And Mamá looked very grave.
But fidgety Phil, he won't sit still;
He wriggles and giggles
And then, I declare,
Swings backward and forward
And tilts up his chair—
Until his chair falls over quite!
Philip screams with all his might,
Catches at the cloth, but then
That makes matters worse again.
Glasses, plates, knives, forks, and all,
Down upon the ground they fall.
Where is Philip? Where is he?
Fairly covered up, you see!
Table all so bare, and ah!
Poor Papá and poor Mamá
Look quite cross, and wonder how
They all shall have their dinner now.

BRITISH ISLES

Jabberwocky
LEWIS CARROLL

'Twas brillig, and the slithy toves
   Did gyre and gimble in the wabe:
All mimsy were the borogoves,
   And the mome raths outgrabe.

"Beware the Jabberwock, my son!
   The jaws that bite, the claws that catch!
Beware the Jubjub bird, and shun
   The frumious Bandersnatch!"

He took his vorpal sword in hand:
   Long time the manxome foe he sought—
So rested he by the Tumtum tree,
   And stood awhile in thought.

And, as in uffish thought he stood,
   The Jabberwock, with eyes of flame,
Came whiffling through the tulgey wood,
   And burbled as it came!

One, two! One, two! And through and through
    The vorpal blade went snicker-snack!
He left it dead, and with its head
    He went galumphing back.

"And hast thou slain the Jabberwock?
    Come to my arms, my beamish boy!
O frabjous day! Callooh! Callay!"
    He chortled in his joy.

'Twas brillig, and the slithy toves
    Did gyre and gimble in the wabe:
All mimsy were the borogoves,
    And the mome raths outgrabe.

Beware the Jabbersock!

Make this Jabberwocky sock puppet and scare all your friends!

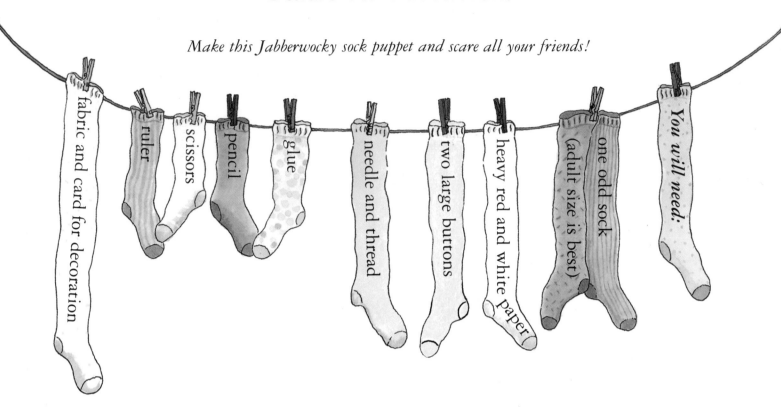

fabric and card for decoration

ruler

scissors

pencil

glue

needle and thread

two large buttons

heavy red and white paper

one odd sock (adult size is best)

You will need:

1. Draw a mouth shape on the red paper. Cut it out and fold it as shown.

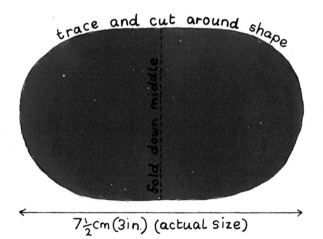

trace and cut around shape

fold down middle

7½cm (3in.) (actual size)

2. Draw the Jabberwocky's teeth on the white paper and cut them out. Fold the lower edge of the teeth over and cut little nicks along the folded edge so that you can curve the teeth around.

fold along line

cut nicks for shaping

fold forwards

10cm (4in.)

3. Cover one side of the red mouth with glue. Push your hand into the sock and make a mouth shape with your fingers at the top and your thumb at the bottom. Stick the red paper into the mouth shape you've made in the sock.

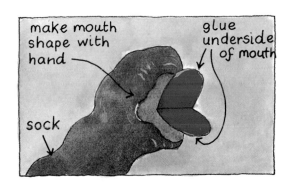

4. Put some glue along the edge of the teeth. Curve the teeth around and stick them onto the puppet's top jaw.

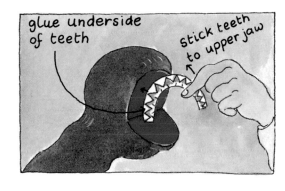

5. When the glue has dried, sew on the two buttons for the Jabberwocky's eyes.

6. Decorate your Jabberwocky by gluing little pieces of cloth or paper onto his body. Make sure he looks really scary!

FRANCE
The Pelican

ROBERT DESNOS

Captain Jonathan
(Aged eighteen the while)
One day caught a pelican
On a far-eastern isle.

In the morning, Jonathan's pelican
Laid an egg, as white as can be;
And from this hatched another pelican
Which resembled the first astonishingly.

This second pelican laid, in turn,
A second egg, as white as can be;
From which, quite inevitably,
Hatched a third, which did the same as she.

And this could go on indefinitely
If you don't make an omelette and eat it for tea.

French Toast

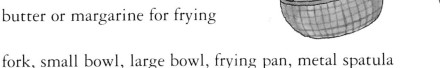

You will need:

3 eggs (hen's eggs will do!)

½ cup milk

1 teaspoon vanilla

8 slices of French bread

(or 4 slices of an ordinary loaf)

butter or margarine for frying

fork, small bowl, large bowl, frying pan, metal spatula

1. In a small bowl, beat the eggs, milk, and vanilla together.

2. Prick the bread well with a fork. Place it in a large bowl.

2. Pour the egg-and-milk mixture over the bread. Keep pricking the bread and turning it with the fork until it has soaked up as much liquid as possible.

3. Melt the butter or margarine in the frying pan over low heat.

4. Put as many slices of bread into the pan as will fit and fry them. Turn them over so they are golden brown on both sides.

5. Remove the French toast from the pan with the spatula and serve it hot with syrup or honey.

The Wedding Gift

If you look up at the sky on a clear night, you can see many different constellations, or groups of stars. The ancient Greeks told stories about how the constellations were created. This is the story of the Northern Crown.

On the shore of the lonely island of Naxos, Ariadne, the princess of Crete, lay sleeping.

The day before, she had helped Theseus kill the Minotaur, a terrifying beast that lived deep in the bewildering maze of passages the Cretans called the Labyrinth. No one could find his way through the Labyrinth without help, so Ariadne had given Theseus a ball of golden thread to take with him. As he went into the maze he unraveled it, then wound it back up to find his way out again.

Then Theseus and Ariadne had escaped to Naxos, where Theseus had promised to marry her. But when Ariadne fell asleep, he sailed away, leaving her all alone.

Ariadne awoke at dawn and saw that the shore was deserted. She could see the silhouette of Theseus's ship disappearing out to sea. She burst into tears, and the sound of her weeping echoed along the empty beach.

Still crying, she wandered sadly over the island, hoping to find houses or perhaps a fisherman who could help her. But after walking all day, she had found no one.

As she walked back to the shore, the air was suddenly filled with light and laughter and the singing of a procession. The god Dionysus was galloping down from the sky in a chariot pulled by two panthers, with his satyrs following behind, dancing and singing noisily.

Dionysus halted his chariot beside Ariadne and took her hand. Speaking to her kindly with words of love, he said, "Weep no more, lovely Ariadne. Come with me and be my queen. We shall live on Mount Olympus, where the gods are already preparing our wedding feast."

Ariadne stepped joyfully into the chariot. Dionysus took the reins, and the procession set off toward the mountain of the gods. As the panthers swept through the darkening sky, Dionysus presented Ariadne with a precious wedding gift—a golden crown encrusted with diamonds and other jewels.

When Ariadne died many years later, Dionysus took her crown and threw it up into the sky. As it rose higher and higher, the gems grew brighter and were turned into stars. We can still see Ariadne's crown gleaming in the sky among the other constellations.

⭐ Make Your Own Star Show ⭐

There are many different constellations in the sky. Which ones you can see depends on where you are in the world and what time of year it is. On a clear night, look up at the night sky and see if you can pick out some of the constellations shown opposite. Then follow the instructions below to make your own star show on your bedroom wall or ceiling.

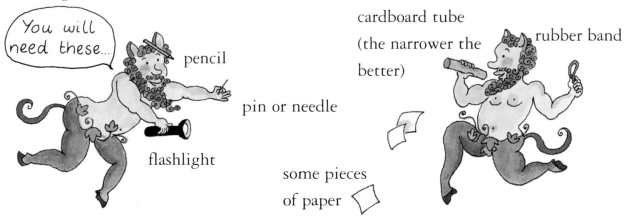

You will need these...

pencil

pin or needle

flashlight

cardboard tube (the narrower the better)

rubber band

some pieces of paper

1. Place a piece of paper over one of the constellations on the opposite page and trace the pattern of the stars with your pencil.
2. Take the pin and make a hole in the paper for each of the stars in the constellation (a big hole for a big star, little holes for smaller stars).
3. Wrap the paper over the end of the cardboard tube and keep it in place with the rubber band.
4. Turn off the light in your room.

The Northern Crown

The Eagle

The Dolphin

5. Turn on the flashlight and hold it inside
the open end of the tube. The light will
shine through the holes in the paper and
project the star pattern onto the wall
or ceiling.

6. Trace some other constellations and
project those, too.

The Crow

The Southern
Crown

Cancer
The Crab

Leo
The Lion

Shrewd Todie and Lyzer the Miser

ISAAC BASHEVIS SINGER

In a village somewhere in the Ukraine there lived a poor man called Todie. Todie had a wife, Sheindel, and seven children, but he could never earn enough to feed them properly. He tried many trades, failing in all of them. It was said of Todie that if he decided to deal in candles the sun would never set. He was nicknamed Shrewd Todie because whenever he managed to make some money, it was always by trickery.

This winter was an especially cold one. The snowfall was heavy and Todie had no money to buy wood for the stove. His seven children stayed in bed all day to keep warm. When the frost burns outside, hunger is stronger than ever, but Sheindel's larder was empty.

In the same village there lived a rich man called Lyzer. Because of his stinginess he was known as Lyzer the miser. He permitted his wife to bake bread only once in four weeks because he had discovered that fresh bread is eaten up more quickly than stale. Todie had more than once gone to Lyzer for a loan of a few gulden, but Lyzer had always replied, "I sleep better when the money lies in my strongbox rather than in your pocket." Todie decided that he would take revenge on Lyzer and at the same time make some much-needed money for himself.

One day, as Lyzer was sitting on a box eating borscht and dry bread (he used his chairs only on holidays so that the upholstery would not wear out), the door opened and Todie came in. "Reb Lyzer," he said, "I would like to ask you a favor. My oldest daughter, Basha, is already fifteen and she's about to become engaged. A young man is coming from Janev to look her over. My cutlery is tin, and my wife is ashamed to ask the young

man to eat soup with a tin spoon. Would you lend me one of your silver spoons? I give you my holy word that I will return it to you tomorrow."

Lyzer knew that Todie would not dare to break a holy oath and he lent him the spoon.

No young man came to see Basha that evening. As usual, the girl walked around barefoot and in rags, and the silver spoon lay hidden under Todie's shirt. In the early years of his marriage Todie had possessed a set of silver tableware himself. He had, however, long since sold it all, with the exception of three silver teaspoons that were used only on Passover. The following day, as Lyzer, his feet bare (in order to save his shoes), sat on his box eating borscht and dry bread, Todie returned.

"Here is the spoon I borrowed yesterday," he said, placing it on the table together with one of his own teaspoons.

"What is the teaspoon for?" Lyzer asked.

And Todie said, "Your tablespoon gave birth to a teaspoon. It is her child. Since I am an honest man, I'm returning both mother and child to you."

Lyzer looked at Todie in astonishment. He had never heard of a silver spoon giving birth to another. Nevertheless, his greed overcame his doubt and he happily accepted both spoons. Such an unexpected piece of good fortune! He was overjoyed that he had loaned Todie the spoon.

A few days later, as Lyzer (without his coat, to save it) was again sitting on his box eating borscht with dry bread, the door opened and Todie appeared. "The young man from Janev did not please Basha, because he had donkey ears, but this evening another young man is coming to look her over. Sheindel is cooking soup for him, but she's ashamed to serve him with a tin spoon. Would you lend me . . ."

Even before Todie could finish the sentence, Lyzer interrupted. "You want to borrow a silver spoon? Take it with pleasure."

The following day Todie once more returned the spoon and with it one of

his own silver teaspoons. He again explained that during the night the large spoon had given birth to a small one and in all good conscience he was bringing back the mother and the newborn baby. As for the young man who had come to look Basha over, she hadn't liked him either, because his nose was so long that it reached to his chin. Needless to say that Lyzer the miser was overjoyed.

Exactly the same thing happened a third time. Todie related that this time his daughter had rejected her suitor because he stammered. He also reported that Lyzer's silver spoon had again given birth to a baby spoon.

"Does it ever happen that a spoon has twins?" Lyzer inquired.

Todie thought it over for a moment. "Why not? I've even heard of a case where a spoon had triplets."

Almost a week passed by and Todie did not go to see Lyzer. But on Friday morning, as Lyzer (in his underdrawers, to save his pants) sat on his box eating borscht and dry bread, Todie came in and said, "Good day to you, Reb Lyzer."

"A good morning and many more to you," Lyzer replied in his friendliest manner. "What good fortune brings you here? Did you perhaps come to borrow a silver spoon? If so, help yourself."

"Today I have a very special favor to ask. This evening a young man from the big city of Lublin is coming to look Basha over. He is the son of a rich man, and I'm told he is clever and handsome as well. Not only do I need a silver spoon, but since he will remain with us over the Sabbath, I need a pair of silver candlesticks, because mine are brass and my wife is ashamed to place them on the Sabbath table. Would you lend me your candlesticks? Immediately after the Sabbath I will return them."

Silver candlesticks are of great value and Lyzer the Miser hesitated, but only for a moment. Remembering his good fortune with the spoons, he said, "I have

46

eight silver candlesticks in my house. Take them all. I know you will return them to me just as you say. And if it should happen that any of them give birth, I have no doubt that you will be as honest as you have been in the past."

"Certainly," Todie said. "Let's hope for the best." The silver spoon, Todie hid beneath his shirt as usual. But taking the candlesticks, he went directly to a merchant, sold them for a considerable sum, and brought the money to Sheindel. When Sheindel saw so much money, she demanded to know where he had gotten such a treasure.

"When I went out, a cow flew over our roof and dropped a dozen silver eggs," Todie replied. "I sold them and here is the money."

"I have never heard of a cow flying over a roof and laying silver eggs," Sheindel said doubtingly.

"There is always a first time," Todie answered. "If you don't want the money, give it back to me."

"There'll be no talk about giving it back," Sheindel said. She knew that her husband was full of cunning and tricks—but when the children are hungry and the larder is empty, it is better not to ask too many questions. Sheindel went to the marketplace and bought meat, fish, white flour, and even some nuts and raisins for a pudding. And since a lot of money still remained, she bought shoes and clothes for the children.

It was a very gay Sabbath in Todie's house. The boys sang and the girls danced. When they asked their father where he had gotten the money, he replied, "It is forbidden to mention money during the Sabbath."

Sunday, as Lyzer (barefoot and almost naked, to save his clothes) sat on his box finishing up a dry crust of bread with borscht, Todie arrived and, handing

Whoa... nice!

Look!

him his silver spoon, said, "It's too bad. This time your spoon did not give birth to a baby."

"What about the candlesticks?" Lyzer inquired anxiously.

Todie sighed deeply. "The candlesticks died."

Lyzer got up from his box so hastily that he overturned his plate of borscht. "You fool! How can candlesticks die?" he screamed.

"If spoons can give birth, candlesticks can die."

Lyzer raised a great hue and cry and had Todie called before the rabbi. When the rabbi heard both sides of the story, he burst out laughing. "It serves you right," he said to Lyzer. "If you hadn't chosen to believe that spoons gave birth, now you would not be forced to believe that your candlesticks died."

"But it's all nonsense," Lyzer objected.

"If you accept nonsense when it brings you profit, you must also accept nonsense when it brings you loss," the rabbi said. And he dismissed the case.

The story spread quickly through the town. All the people enjoyed Todie's victory and Lyzer the miser's defeat. The shoemaker's and tailor's apprentices made up a song about it.

However, time passed and Lyzer's silver spoons never gave birth again.

Lyzer, put your grief aside. What if your candlesticks have died? You're the richest man on earth with silver spoons that can give birth...

...and silver eggs as living proof of flying cows above your roof. Don't sit there eating crusts of bread— To silver grandsons look ahead!

Shrewd Todie's Potato Latkes

Latkes are a traditional Jewish recipe. They are crispy potato cakes that are delicious either hot or cold. This recipe makes ten latkes.

You will need:

3 medium potatoes

1 egg

pinch of salt and pepper

3 tablespoons vegetable oil for frying

1 small onion

potato peeler, grater, 2 large bowls, fork, sieve, frying pan, tablespoon, spatula, paper towels

1. Peel the potatoes, then grate them. Put the grated potato into a bowl of cold water to keep it from turning brown.
2. Peel and grate the onion.
3. In a bowl, beat the egg with a fork. Add the onion, salt, and pepper and beat the whole mixture again.
4. Drain the grated potato in a sieve. Shake it well to get rid of as much water as possible. Add it to the egg mixture and stir well.
5. Put the oil in a frying pan and heat it on the stove. Ask an adult to help you.
6. Put tablespoons of the mixture into the pan and press them flat.
7. Fry the latkes for about five minutes on each side, using a metal spatula to turn them over.
8. Lift them carefully onto paper towels to drain off the oil. Serve hot with applesauce or sour cream.

The Captain's Goose

Scandinavia is the name given to the area that comprises the countries of Norway, Sweden, Denmark, Finland, and Iceland.

Once upon a time, long, long ago, there was a famous sea captain. His very name made pirates tremble, because he was their sworn enemy and killed them off like flies. But good men had nothing to fear from him, and he was always kind and ready to help them. As a result, everyone loved him, and kings were pleased to see him wherever he visited.

One day he was on board his ship, feeling rather hungry and waiting for his cook to finish cooking him a goose. Quite out of the blue, Piers the Magician appeared in his cabin and said, "Captain, I have heard many good things about you, and I would like to do you a good turn. Tell me, would you like to be a king?"

"I've never really thought about it," the captain replied calmly.

"Then think about it now," said Piers. "If you had the choice, would you rather be a king or a captain?"

"A king, I think," said the captain. "In fact, a king, definitely."

"Quite right," said Piers. "And would you reward the man who made you a king?"

"I would," said the captain.

"Would you give him ten kroner a year?"

"A hundred," said the captain. "At the very least."

"You're very kind," said Piers. "But ten kroner is all I ask."

"My friend, it will be yours," the captain promised, and, their bargain struck, they parted. The captain went to check on his goose, which was not quite ready, while Piers set off on a long journey.

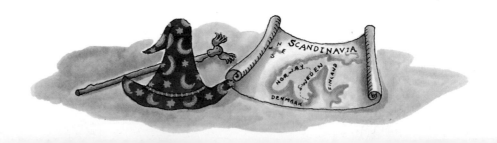

After many hours, Piers came to a city where the king had just died, leaving behind his kingdom, his queen, and his baby son. The courtiers had just decided that the little boy should become king when Piers stepped in.

"My lords," he said, "is he not a little young to cope with the terrible task that awaits him?"

"What terrible task?" they asked.

"Have you not heard?" said Piers.

"Heard what?" they asked.

"About all the pirate ships that have just docked at port, full of pirates—armed to the teeth and greedy for gold!"

The courtiers ran to the watchtowers and saw that what Piers had said was true. "These pirates will seize our baby king and carry off our queen and not leave a soul alive in the city!" they wailed. "What is to be done?" they asked Piers. And Piers told them.

"There is only one thing to do: you must find a brave sea captain to rule you," he said. "And as it happens, I know just the man. He is so brave and so fierce toward pirates that you will not find anyone like him from here to the ends of the earth. Will you take him?"

The courtiers said they would. So Piers traveled back to where the brave sea captain was waiting, with his sword in one hand and a brand-new cloak in the other, and already looking the very picture of a king. Piers told him that he could become a king that very day if he would keep his promise to pay him ten kroner a year.

"My friend, it is yours," vowed the captain, and—clink, clink, clink—down came the money in Piers's hand.

They reached the city later that day. Before he'd even had time to shake the dust from his boots, the captain was crowned and had married the queen, adopted the little prince, and begun to learn his new profession.

The moment the pirates heard that the new king was none other than their sworn enemy, they fled for their lives and were not seen again. The courtiers were very pleased.

"What a good king we chose!" they said.

So the king's first year passed in peace. Then, one year later to the very day, Piers came back to the palace to see him. The king was up to his eyes with ruling, but delighted to see the magician all the same.

"I am here for my ten kroner," said Piers.

"My friend," said the king, "I have it ready." And he clinked out the money into his friend's hand—clink, clink, clink—ten times over.

The courtiers thought this was very strange. "Why is it his and not ours?" they wondered.

So when, a year later to the day, Piers walked in a second time and the king clinked out ten more kroner, the courtiers thought it was even more odd.

They began to wonder why a stranger should be asking tribute of their king, and why their king should be clinking away the coffers of the city, doing no one any good—except, of course, the stranger. They murmured among themselves that they would rather the magician left their city for good.

When the king heard these rumors, he was worried. After all, he saw Piers only once a year, but he saw his courtiers every day, and he didn't want to offend them. So he spoke to Piers:

"My friend," he said. "You don't want to be bothered with coming all this way every year. Why not skip your visit next year? And perhaps the year after that as well," he added, hoping Piers would take the hint.

But the magician just said, "You can expect me at the usual time," and off he went with his money.

When, a year later to the day, Piers walked in a third time and asked for his ten kroner, the king became very cross. In fact, he completely lost his temper.

"Of all the impertinence!" he cried. "Would you abuse my kindness? I will not stand for this behavior! Leave my court this instant!"

"Certainly," said Piers. "When you have paid me my ten kroner."

"Traitor!" screamed the king. "Bind him! Punish him! Throw him into the dungeon!"

"When you have quite finished your temper tantrum," said Piers, "may I remind you of something?"

"Of what?" snapped the king.

"Of the bargain we made while your goose was cooking," said Piers.

"I remember the goose, certainly," said the king. "It smelled marvelous, although it wasn't quite cooked, as I recall."

"Let me refresh your memory," said Piers. "Then you were only a sea captain, and you were kind and generous and trustworthy. But now that you are a king you are unjust and greedy and not true to your word. So because you have now shown yourself in your true colors: *King, your goose is cooked!*"

To the king's astonishment, when he looked about him, everything had vanished: palace, courtiers, Piers, and all. He was back on his ship, a sea captain again. His three royal years were all a dream. A wiser—and hungrier— man than he had been before, he called for his goose (which was, indeed, now cooked) and ate it.

And that is how the saying "Your goose is cooked" came to be, and why, if your goose is cooked, you may find you have learned a painful, but useful, lesson.

The Captain's Treasure Chest

When sailors went to sea, they often decorated a box with shells to give to their loved ones back home. If you have lots of shells, you could make a shell box to give as a present. Or use other decorations to make a treasure chest fit for a king.

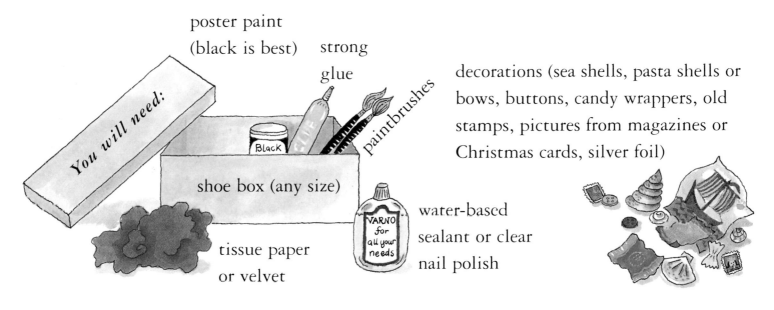

poster paint (black is best)

strong glue

paintbrushes

decorations (sea shells, pasta shells or bows, buttons, candy wrappers, old stamps, pictures from magazines or Christmas cards, silver foil)

You will need:

shoe box (any size)

water-based sealant or clear nail polish

tissue paper or velvet

1. Paint the outside of the shoe box and lid. Allow to dry.
2. When the box is dry, plan your decoration by laying the collage on the box and lid without gluing anything down.
3. Glue the decorations firmly onto the lid and sides of the box. (Don't stick decorations too far up the sides or you won't be able to close the lid.)
4. When everything is completely dry, carefully brush or spray a clear, water-based sealant over the whole box.
5. When the sealant is dry, line the inside of the box with tissue paper, velvet, or some silky material and fill it with treasure!

Peter and the Wolf

Based on the musical story by SERGEI PROKOFIEV

Early one morning Peter opened the garden gate and went out into the great green meadow.

He went over to the tree where his friend, the little bird, was sitting.

"All is quiet!" chirped the bird happily. "All is well."

Peter and the bird were still talking when a duck came waddling out of the woods to have a quiet swim in the meadow pond.

When the little bird saw her swimming, he started to tease her. "How can you call yourself a bird when you can't even fly?" he taunted.

"How can you call yourself a bird when you can't even swim?" replied the duck, and she dived under the water.

And so they continued, the bird chirping on the bank and the duck answering back from the pond; and they were so wrapped up in their argument that they never saw the danger approaching.

It was the cat! Very softly she padded toward them. When she was close enough, she gathered herself, ready to pounce.

In the nick of time, Peter saw her. "Look out!" he shouted, and the bird flew up into the tree.

The duck, sitting safely in the middle of the pond, quacked angrily at the cat, but the cat ignored her and paced around and around the tree.

"By the time I climb up there the bird will have flown away," she thought.

At that moment Peter's grandfather came out of the house. He hurried toward them, angry that Peter had gone into the meadow.

"Come here this minute!" he called. "How often must I tell you that the meadow is a dangerous place! A wolf could come out of the forest at any time. Then what would you do?"

"I'd soon deal with him!" said Peter, who wasn't afraid of wolves.

"I think he'd soon deal with you!" scolded Grandfather. He took Peter by the hand, led him home, and locked the high gate firmly behind them.

As they walked away, a big gray wolf came out of the forest.

The bird saw him first and shrilled a warning. In a twinkling, the cat shot up the tree and perched next to the bird. But the duck wasn't so sensible. Instead of staying safely in the water, she squawked and quacked and flapped, and in her panic jumped right out of the pond.

The wolf was very near now, and the duck tried to run. But no matter how fast she ran, she couldn't escape. The wolf's great jaws snapped closer and closer until, in one gulp, he swallowed her whole!

The hungry wolf now turned his attention to the cat and the bird. He crept around and around the tree, looking up at them greedily as they crouched in the branches above him.

All this time, Peter had stood fearlessly behind the closed gate, watching. Now he ran home to get a strong rope. He climbed up the high stone wall. One of the branches of the tree stretched out over the wall. Peter grabbed hold of it and climbed lightly into the tree.

He called softly to the bird, "Fly down and flutter around the wolf's head. Just take care that he doesn't catch you."

The bird flew so close to the wolf that he almost touched the wolf's nose with his wings. The wolf was desperate to catch him and snapped angrily at him from this side and that. But the little bird was too quick and too clever, and always kept just out of reach.

While the wolf wasn't looking, Peter made a lasso with his rope. Without a sound, he lowered it down over the wolf's tail, and then he pulled with all his might. The wolf was caught!

Snap!

He jumped and flailed wildly, trying to get free. But Peter tied the other end of the rope to the tree, and the more the wolf jumped, the tighter the rope became.

The wolf's howls of rage brought Grandfather out of the house, and he stared in amazement at the scene. Then some hunters came out of the woods, following the wolf's trail and shooting as they went.

Peter called out to them, "Don't shoot! The little bird and I have caught the wolf. Help us take him to the zoo."

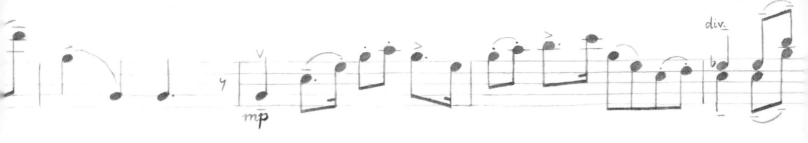

And off they went in a triumphant procession!

Peter strode along in front, with the hunters leading the wolf behind them. Then came Grandfather, very proud of Peter, but still shaking his head and muttering, "What if Peter hadn't caught the wolf? Then what would have happened?"

The cat brought up the rear, and the little bird flew above them all, chirping merrily, "How brave we are! Look what we have caught!"

And if you had listened very carefully, you could have heard the duck quacking, because the wolf, in his hurry, had swallowed her alive!

Peter and the Wolf Finger Puppets

Grr...

Quack! Tweet!

Miaow!

Show here tonight 6 o'clock

You will need:

paper

pencil

crayons or felt-tip pens

scissors

transparent tape

STARRING wolf, cat, bird, duck and... Peter! Co-starring hunters and Grandfather

1. Put the paper over the pictures on these pages and carefully trace around the outlines with a pencil.
2. Color in the pictures with crayons or felt-tip pens.
3. Carefully cut around the thick outlines with scissors.
4. Take one puppet and bend the tabs on its base around two of your fingers. Fasten the tabs together with tape.
5. Repeat with each of the other puppets.
6. Now you're ready to act out *Peter and the Wolf*!

Peter

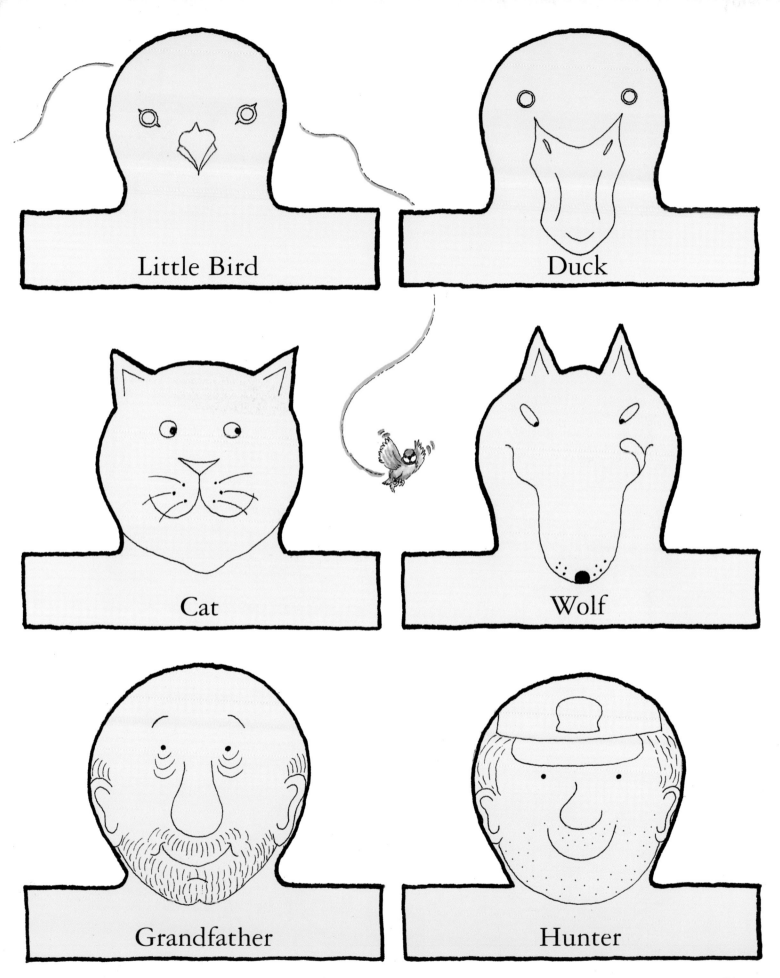

Little Bird

Duck

Cat

Wolf

Grandfather

Hunter

Haiku

The haiku is a special type of poem that was invented in Japan hundreds of years ago. The poems are just one sentence long, but they are much harder to write than they look. Even though they are so short, good haiku can often convey much more vivid images or ideas than long, elaborate descriptions.

Year's end—
still in straw hat
and sandals.

Basho

Autumn—
even the birds
and clouds look old.

Basho

Old pond,
leap-splash—
a frog.

Basho

Above the boat,
bellies of
wild geese.

Kikaku

One sneeze—
skylark's
out of sight.

Yayu

Moonlit night—
by melon flowers,
fox sneezes.

Shirao

One bath
after another—
how stupid.

Issa

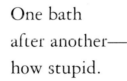

Clouds of mosquitoes—
it would be bare
without them.

Issa

Summer sky
clear after rain—
ants on parade.

Shiki

Japanese Fish Kite

Japanese children make these kites to celebrate Children's Day.
They fly them outside or hang them from their windows.

This is what you'll need...

large plastic trash bag or large
sheets of colored tissue paper

crayons, scissors, rubber cement or
white glue, pipe cleaners (at least
10 inches long), kite string

things to decorate your kite—sequins,
glitter, colored paper, stickers

1. With a crayon, draw a shape
on the trash bag as shown in the
picture on the right (if you are
using colored tissue paper, fold
the paper in half lengthwise first—
but don't crease it). Cut through
both layers at once.

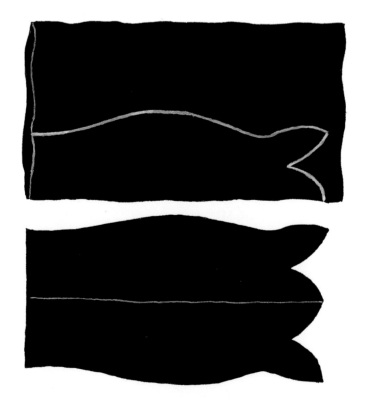

2. Cut around the shape and then open it out so that it looks like the picture on the right.

3. Put a line of glue along the short, straight edge of the shape.

4. Put a pipe cleaner next to the glue. Fold the glued plastic over the pipe cleaner and press it down firmly.

5. Turn the kite over. The side facing you will be the outside of the kite.

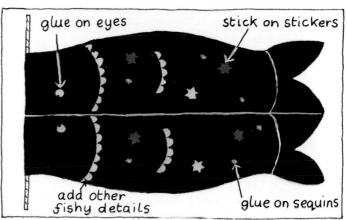

6. Decorate this side all over by gluing on glitter, sequins, pieces of paper, or anything else you like. Remember, this is a fish kite, so you can give it eyes, scales, and fins.

7. Carefully pick the kite up by the pipe cleaner. Bend the pipe cleaner to form a circle and twist the ends together.

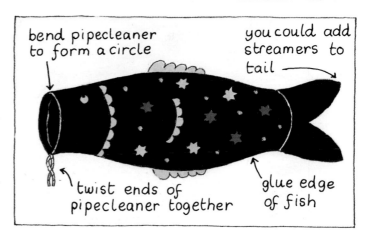

8. Run a line of glue along the inside of the fish's belly. Fold the fish so that the long edges of the belly stick firmly together. Leave the tail end of the fish open.

9. Tie a length of kite string to the ends of the pipe cleaner by the mouth of the fish. To fly your kite outside, make a handle by tying the other end of the string to a long bamboo pole. You could also just pin the string to your window frame and watch your kite blow in the breeze.

The Story of the Willow Pattern Plate

The blue and white willow pattern has been a popular design on plates and china for hundreds of years. Through its pictures, the pattern tells a dramatic story.

Long ago in old China, there was a wealthy mandarin who lived in a beautiful house surrounded by trees. He had just one child—a beautiful daughter named Koong-see. He also had a brilliant young secretary named Chang. Koong-see and Chang were very much in love, but they dared not tell the mandarin of their feelings because Chang was poor. Each evening they would meet secretly in the orange grove by the house and dream of the day when Chang would be rich and they could marry.

Then, one day, the mandarin heard of their meetings. In his fury he banished Chang from his estate and built a fence across the footpath to his house. Then he betrothed Koong-see to a wealthy ta-jin, a duke of high degree, who was almost as old as he was.

To prevent Koong-see from running after Chang, the mandarin locked her in a building by the water's edge. He told her that her wedding to the ta-jin would take place when the peach tree bloomed in the spring. From her prison, Koong-see could see the willow tree already in flower, but the peach tree, to her relief, had barely formed its buds.

Weeks passed, and Koong-see sadly watched the willow blossoms wither while the buds swelled on the peach tree. Then one day, a little boat made out of a coconut shell floated past her window. In it she found a message from Chang, urging her to be brave and to get ready to escape.

Not long after, the ta-jin paid a state visit to the mandarin to make the final arrangements for the wedding.

The ta-jin was attended by so great a retinue of soldiers and servants that Chang was able to slip in among them. While the mandarin and the ta-jin were feasting, Chang found Koong-see, and they fled away together across the bridge beside the willow tree. Koong-see carried her distaff, Chang the box of jewels that had been the ta-jin's wedding gift.

They were soon spotted by the mandarin, who came after them with a whip. But the young lovers were too swift for him, and they managed to hide in the gardener's cottage on the other side of the bridge.

When the ta-jin heard what had happened, he was furious and swore that the lovers should die. He sent his soldiers to search every house for miles around. But when the soldiers came to the gardener's cottage, Koong-see and Chang jumped out of a window into a boat. They sailed hundreds of miles away to a distant island, where they married.

On the island they could finally live in peace. Chang devoted himself to writing, and his books made his fortune. Soon he was able to build Koong-see a fine house fit for the daughter of a mandarin. Chang also became famous throughout China for his great wisdom and learning—so famous, in fact, that the ta-jin came to hear of him. Still consumed with wrath and determined to have his revenge, he ordered his soldiers to sail down the great river and attack the island where Chang and Koong-see lived.

The young couple were killed defending their home, but their story did not end there. They were transformed into two immortal doves, flying high for all to see, symbols of the undying love that two people can have for each other.

Decorate a Plate

pencil

paintbrushes

eraser

You will need...

paper plate

...but not a shiny laminated one!

poster paints

Whoops!

or crayons

or felt-tip pens

water-based sealant

or clear nail polish

1. Decide what scene you want to paint on your plate. You could do a drawing of a family holiday or something exciting you have done, or try illustrating a nursery rhyme or poem.

2. Sketch your design on the plate with the pencil. Use the flat part of the plate for your story and the edges for a decorative border.

3. Color in your design with paint, crayons, or felt-tip pens. You could use lots of different colors or, as with the Willow Pattern, just one color. If you use paint, allow it to dry completely before going on to step 4.

4. Use a different paintbrush to varnish the plate, or spray on a clear, water-based sealant. Allow the plate to dry.

Can you guess the story?

It's in this book!

AUSTRALIA

Waltzing Matilda

Once a jolly swagman camped by a billabong,
    Under the shade of a coolabah tree,
And he sang as he watched and waited till his billy boiled,
    "Who'll come a-waltzing Matilda with me?"

Waltzing Matilda, waltzing Matilda,
    Who'll come a-waltzing Matilda with me?
And he sang as he watched and waited till his billy boiled,
    "Who'll come a-waltzing Matilda with me?"

Down came a jumbuck to drink at the billabong,
    Up jumped the swagman and grabbed him with glee;
And he sang as he stowed that jumbuck in his tucker-bag,
    "You'll come a-waltzing Matilda with me!"

Down came the squatter, riding on his thoroughbred,
    Down came the troopers—one, two, and three.
"Where's that jolly jumbuck you've got in your tucker-bag?
    You'll come a-waltzing Matilda with me!"

Up jumped the swagman and plunged into the billabong.
    "You'll never catch me alive," cried he.
And his ghost may be heard as you pass by that billabong,
    "You'll come a-waltzing Matilda with me!"

Who'll come a-waltzing Matilda with me?

The Swagman's Hat

You will need:
large piece of cardboard
scissors
pencil
skewer or knitting needle
yarn or string
lots of small objects (corks, thread spools, buttons, beads) to decorate your hat

1. Draw a large circle on the cardboard, about 16 inches across. Cut it out.
2. In the center, cut out a smaller circle, big enough to fit onto your head (about 6 ½ inches across).
3. Use the skewer or knitting needle to make holes all around the edge of the circle. Put a stack of newspapers or several layers of cardboard underneath the circle as you push the skewer through so that you don't damage the table.
4. Cut lots of pieces of yarn or string about 6 inches long.
5. Thread your decorations on the pieces of string.
6. Push each piece of string through one of the holes in the brim of your hat and tie a knot in the end.
7. Your swagman's hat is ready to wear!

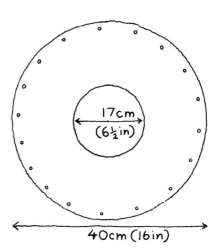

17cm (6½in)

40cm (16in)

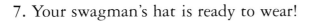

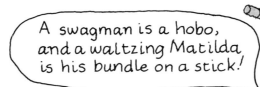

A swagman is a hobo, and a waltzing Matilda is his bundle on a stick!

The Monkey and the Crocodile

On the bank of a big river grew a splendid mango tree, which produced such an abundance of fruit that its branches were bowed down and their tips dragged in the water. In that tree lived a monkey. Down below, in the river, lived a great many crocodiles.

Each day, the monkey feasted on mangoes from his tree. He was not a careful eater, and several mangoes would fall into the river to rot or be carried away on the strong, slow current.

One of the crocodiles saw this happening and decided to try some of the mangoes that were washed into his lurking place near the riverbank. The fruit was sweet and juicy—as splendid as the tree from which it fell. It was dull green on the outside but glorious orange within, the color of the sun. The crocodile started to wait beneath the tree when he knew the monkey would be eating, and soon the two became friends.

From that day forth they would spend all day long chattering together and eating mangoes until the sun sank in the sky. Then the crocodile would remember his wife and family and would lumber slowly home.

The crocodile's wife became suspicious of her husband's long absences and sent one of her children to spy on him. When she heard how he was spending all day eating mangoes with a monkey, she was enraged, and determined to have her revenge.

When her husband came home that night, she pretended to be very ill. She lay in bed, groaning as if she would die. The father crocodile was most concerned. "Be brave," he told her. "I shall fetch the doctor at once."

But his wife called him back. "It's no use," she cried weakly. "I have seen a doctor. He said I'll be cured only if I eat the heart of a monkey."

The father crocodile started to panic.

"But I don't know where to find a monkey's heart!" he protested.

"What do you mean?" asked his wife, her voice sinking to a whisper. "Do you not eat mangoes with a monkey every day? Does that monkey not have a heart? Such a sweet heart, fed every day with mangoes, would be sure to cure me right away."

"But that monkey is my friend! I cannot kill my friend." The father crocodile was almost weeping.

At this the mother crocodile turned blue with anger. "You don't mind if I die, but you can't bear the thought of your friend dying?" She started to cry, and so did all their children, gathered around her bed.

Now the father crocodile was at his wits' end. He knew that the monkey must die but could not think how to kill him. His wife came to his aid.

"I have a plan," she said, still gasping as if in great pain. "You must invite the monkey to dinner. Then we will kill him, and I will be cured."

Very sadly, the father crocodile did as he was told. When he arrived at the mango tree, he called to his friend. "My wife has been very sick," he said, "but now she is better, and we would like you to come and dine with us to celebrate."

"I should be delighted to," said the monkey. "But how shall I get there? I cannot swim."

"Do not worry," the crocodile reassured him. "I shall carry you on my back. You will be quite safe. . . ." But his voice trailed away, for he knew that his friend would not be safe at all.

When they were in mid-river, with the monkey clinging to his back, the crocodile decided that he must tell the truth. Guiltily, he explained about his wife's illness and how she must eat a monkey's heart. "I am sorry, my friend, but there is no other way. I must kill you to save my wife. Please forgive me."

The monkey had to think fast, for they were nearly at the crocodile's home, and he did not want to die.

"My good friend!" he exclaimed. "Of course I forgive

you. But you should have told me the truth before we set off. I left my heart back in the mango tree, hanging on a branch. I never imagined that I'd need it. Don't worry—if you take me back quickly I can fetch it, and your wife will be made well."

The crocodile agreed and swam swiftly back to the bank. When they arrived, the monkey leaped nimbly up into his tree, well out of reach. Then he turned to the crocodile and shouted, "Ha! My *dearest* friend! To save your wife's life you lied to me and played a trick on me. Now to save my life I have lied and played a trick on you. I never left my heart on a branch! It was beating safely in my body all along."

And these were the last words the monkey ever spoke to the crocodile. From that day forth, the monkey was careful to drop no more mangoes as he ate. Instead, he kept them until their green skin turned black and their orange flesh was brown and rotten, and then he would throw them at the crocodile as he swam past, laughing as the missiles hit their mark.

As for the crocodile, he returned to his family very confused, to find his wife fully recovered and preparing a fine dinner to welcome him.

Monkey's Mango Lassi

Lassi is an Indian yogurt drink. You can also make it with other kinds of fruit—try peaches, pineapple, or bananas.

You will need:

large mango (or one 5-ounce can of mangoes)

10 fluid ounces of natural yogurt

2–3 tablespoons of sugar or honey

¼ teaspoon of ground cardamom seeds (optional)

8 ice cubes

peeler or sharp knife, cutting board,

blender, glasses

1. Peel the mango and throw away the big pit in the middle. If you're using canned mangoes, drain off the juice and just use the fruit.
2. Chop up the mango.
3. Put the chopped mango in an electric blender with all the other ingredients and blend them together. (The ice cubes may not get completely ground up, but it doesn't matter if some pieces remain.)
4. Pour the lassi into two or three glasses and serve.

The Great Round

Greenland

Canada

United States of America

Start here

0

1

Sea serpent chases ship

2

Go back to beginning.

3

Giant blows ship along.

4

Go forward 3

Caribbean

Crew eats too many bananas.

13

Go back two.

14

15

16

Follow pelican eastwards on to no. 35.

17

19

20

British Isles

Scandinavia

France

12

11

Dolphins follow ship. Good omen.

10

Take extra turn.

South America

5

Captain's parrot gets sunstroke.

6

miss a turn.

7

8

Go forward one

9

Good navigation around rocks.

N
W — E
S

what you will need to play:
One die
One counter for each person

How to play
Take turns to throw the die and follow the numbers. First one to finish gets the treasure!

Yellow squares help you along.
Watch out for the red squares - they're dangerous!